AMERICAN
WOMEN
OF MEDICINE

The Collective Biographies Series

Collective Biographies

AMERICAN WOMEN OF MEDICINE

Russell Roberts

Enslow Publishers, Inc.

40 Industrial Road	PO Box 38
Box 398	Aldershot
Berkeley Heights, NJ 07922	Hants GU12 6BP
USA	UK

http://www.enslow.com

Library of Congress Cataloging-in-Publication Data

Roberts, Russell, 1953-
    American women of medicine / Russell Roberts.
      p. cm.—(Collective biographies)
    Includes bibliographical references and index.
    Summary: Discusses the lives and the struggles faced by ten women who pursued careers in the medical field, including Dorothea Lynde Dix, Elizabeth Blackwell, Clara Barton, Mary Edwards Walker, Susie King Taylor, Susan LaFlesche Picotte, Clara Maass, Gerty Radnitz Cori, Antonia Coello Novello, and Mae Carol Jemison.
    ISBN 0-7660-1835-0
    1. Women in medicine—United States—Biography—Juvenile literature. [1. Women in medicine. 2. Women—Biography]   I. Title.
    R692 . R63 2002
    610'.82'0973—dc21   2001003475

Printed in the United States of America

10 9 8 7 6 5 4 3 2 1

To Our Readers:
We have done our best to make sure all Internet Addresses in this book were active and appropriate when we went to press. However, the author and the publisher have no control over and assume no liability for the material available on those Internet sites or on other Web sites they may link to. Any comments or suggestions can be sent by e-mail to comments@enslow.com or to the address on the back cover.

Every effort has been made to locate all copyright holders of material used in this book. If any errors or omissions have occurred, corrections will be made in future editions of this book.

Illustration Credits: Bristol-Myers, Squibb, 67, Library of Congress, 8, 14, Library of Medicine, 16, 62, 70, 76, NARA (National Archives), 26, 32, 34, 37, 49, NASA, 88, 93, Program Support Center, Department of Health and Human Services, 80, 85, Schomburg Center for Research in Black Culture, 44, Smithsonian Institute, 54, 59, Warren Hunting Smith Library, Hobart & William Smith Colleges, 21.

Cover Illustration: NASA, Program Support Center, Department of Health and Human Services, Library of Medicine.

Contents

Preface

Ten extraordinary women risked ridicule, poverty, gossip, and even their lives in pursuit of their dreams to help others.

How can I help people who suffer illness? What ingredient can I include to create a cure? How can I improve the way people with illness are cared for?

These are just some of the questions women of medicine asked. Simply asking "why" knocked down barriers, facilitated medical breakthroughs and improved the lives of the sick and abandoned. Their gratitude, in many cases, only consisted of a sense of personal satisfaction. However, their tenacity despite little or no recognition created a haven for the sick and a stepping stone for the future of women in medicine.

Oftentimes, making the choice to pursue medicine lead to a lifetime of scorn. Nevertheless, their refusal to leave things unchallenged ultimately made the world a better place for those who suffer. History defines these women as the trailblazers of women in medicine.

Mary Edwards Walker was the first woman to receive the Congressional Medal of Freedom for her efforts to help soldiers during the Civil War. Susan LaFlesche Picotte was the first American Indian doctor and she traveled hundreds of miles across all kinds of weather to help sick people who had no other access to doctors or medicine. Antonio Novello became the first Hispanic Surgeon General of the United States, and Susie King Taylor risked her life to nurse soldiers of all colors despite the cruelty she suffered through racial discrimination. And of course there's Elizabeth Blackwell, the first female doctor who opened the door for them all.

These and other amazing women are all present in this book. Their stories are filled with joy, triumphs, courage, and pain.

Young Clara Maass courageously bared her arm to a mosquito carrying yellow fever disease. Gerty Cori overcame sexual bias and was the first American woman to win a Nobel Prize for Medicine for her research on the effect of sugar on the human body. And finally, Clara Barton, the shy, but determined young woman, who founded the American Red Cross.

Dorothea Dix

Dorothea Lynde Dix
(1802–1887)

At the age of thirty-five, Dorothea Dix, a former schoolteacher, inherited enough money so that she would never need to work again. But while many people would have used such an inheritance to live a life of luxury, Dix did not.

Using the money to support herself, Dix devoted her life to improving conditions for the mentally ill.

Dorothea Lynde Dix was born April 4, 1802, on a farm near the town of Hampden in Maine. Her childhood was far from idyllic and she said later, "I never knew childhood."[1]

One reason had to do with her unstable father, Joseph Dix. As a student at Harvard University, he had angered his parents by rejecting their Calvinist religion and becoming a follower of a street preacher named Charles Wesley.

Then, over his parents' strong objections, Dix married Mary Bigelow, a poor woman who was eighteen years older than he was.

Joseph Dix was promptly expelled from Harvard because the university did not allow students to be married. His father sent the couple to the family-owned farm in Maine. He hoped that his son would help persuade people to settle in what was essentially a wilderness area.

But instead of settling down, Joseph Dix became more erratic. He drank heavily, which caused arguments and provoked violence between the couple. He wrote long, rambling religious essays, which Dorothea and her mother had to sew and paste together for him.

When she was twelve, Dorothea was sent to live with her wealthy grandmother in Boston. But wealth did not equal affection. Her grandmother, who saw to Dorothea's education and training, was a harsh disciplinarian.

At the age of fourteen, Dorothea moved to Worcester, Massachusetts, to live with a great-aunt. While there, Dorothea opened a school for small children. Several years later her grandmother gave Dorothea permission to establish a school for wealthy children—mainly young girls—at her large Boston home.

Dorothea began her school at the Dix mansion on April 2, 1821. She was a serious and responsible young woman who was described as "tall and dignified, but stooped somewhat . . . very shy in her manners, and colored [blushed] extremely when addressed."[2]

Dix threw herself into her work with fierce dedication. She even turned down a marriage proposal because she feared that marriage would interfere with her work.

Dix drove herself hard; she was always reading, studying, and planning for her students. When her grandmother fell ill, Dix took on the extra work of caring for her as well.

Dix pushed herself to the point of mental and physical exhaustion. "There is so much to do, I am broken on a wheel," she wrote to a friend.[3]

Finally, in early 1836, everything caught up with Dix. She suffered a complete mental and physical collapse and lost the use of one lung. She was forced to close her school.

Dix sailed to Liverpool, England, where she spent the next eighteen months recuperating at the home of one of her doctor's friends. For the first time in her life she truly relaxed. She later called this period the "jubilee of her life."[4]

On April 29, 1837, Dix's grandmother died and left Dix a comfortable income. Dix now had enough money so she would never have to work again.

One day in March 1841, while Dix was walking home from church, she overheard two men behind her talking. They were discussing the terrible conditions that poor people who were mentally ill had to endure in the jail in East Cambridge, Massachusetts.

Dix visited the jail and was appalled at what she saw. The mentally-ill people were in one large, dirty, unheated room. When she asked why there was no stove to keep them warm, she was told that "lunatics didn't feel the cold."

That attitude was typical of how poor mentally-ill people in the United States were treated at the time. Since they couldn't fight for better conditions for themselves, Dix decided to adopt their cause and fight for them.

Dix's crusade began with a small victory. She publicized through the newspapers the terrible conditions in the East Cambridge jail. She was rewarded when a local court ordered that the mentally-ill men and women confined there should receive a stove.

Having triumphed locally, Dix decided to investigate what conditions were like for the mentally ill throughout the state of Massachusetts.

In January 1843, Dix completed her investigation. She wrote a report called a Memorial to the Legislature of Massachusetts, which she submitted to the Massachusetts legislators.

In her report Dix detailed the squalid, inhuman conditions of the prisons and poorhouses in the state where the mentally ill were kept with criminals. The mentally ill were "thrown into cages, closets, cellars, stalls, pens and chained, beaten with rods, and lashed into obedience," she wrote.[5]

After describing these conditions, Dix challenged the Massachusetts legislature to correct them. "I beg. I implore. I demand pity and protection for these of my suffering, outraged sex," she wrote.[6]

The memorial was such a powerful and compelling document that it provoked public outrage. It swept aside any opposition. The Massachusetts legislature passed a bill ordering that the Worcester State Hospital provide accommodations for an additional two hundred mentally-ill people.

Dorothea Dix had found her life's work. She began visiting other states, observing the deplorable conditions in which the mentally ill were housed. Then she described these conditions in a written memorial to each state's legislature.

In the next few years, thanks to her urging and pleas, the states of Rhode Island and New York improved conditions for the mentally ill.

In 1843, Dix took her crusade to New Jersey, which had neither private nor public facilities for the mentally ill. In January 1845, Dix presented her written memorial to the New Jersey legislature.

Two months later the New Jersey legislature, which had resisted all attempts to spend any money for the mentally ill, voted overwhelmingly to establish a state hospital for their care.

This was the first time that Dix's efforts had been responsible for the construction of an entirely new facility. Thereafter, she referred to the New Jersey hospital as her "firstborn" child.

Dorothea Dix founded this Soldiers' Home in Washington, D.C., to help wounded soldiers during and after the Civil War. It is now known as the Army Veteran Hospital.

Ultimately, Dix was responsible for founding institutions or improving conditions for mentally-ill poor people in twenty states, as well as in Canada.

She traveled thousands of miles alone on roads that were little more than dirt trails. This would have been difficult for a completely healthy woman; for a person with one lung like Dix, it must have been horrendous.

For six years, from 1848 to 1854, Dix worked strenuously to get Congress to pass a bill that would distribute 5 million acres of federal land to the states for the purpose of building hospitals to care for the mentally ill. Finally, in 1854, Congress passed a bill setting aside 10 million acres for this purpose.

Dix's jubilation was short-lived, however, for President Franklin Pierce, who had initially expressed his support, vetoed it. He voted against it on the grounds that it was unconstitutional for the federal government to make land grants for charitable causes.

In June 1861, when Dix was nearly sixty years old, she was appointed superintendent of Union Army nurses just after the Civil War began. Her job was to select and assign women nurses to military hospitals.

Dix was used to working alone and found it difficult to delegate authority. Widely criticized for her almost dictatorial methods, Dix one day cried out in frustration, "This is not the work I would have my life judged by!"[7]

When the war was over, Dix asked for nothing from the federal government for her years of service except the "flag of my country."[8] This request was granted.

Dix resumed her work on behalf of the mentally ill. But by now, she was sickly and frail and weighed just ninety-five pounds. She frequently fell ill on her investigative tours and had to take long rests to recover.

In October 1881, while on a visit to the New Jersey State Hospital she helped found, Dix fell ill and could not travel any longer. The managers of the hospital, grateful for all Dix had done, prepared a special apartment for her in the hospital.

Dix spent the remainder of her days there, sheltered and cared for within the halls of her beloved "firstborn." Dorothea Lynde Dix died on July 17, 1887, at the age of eighty-five.

As one of her many friends wrote: She was "the most useful and distinguished woman America has yet produced."[9]

Elizabeth Blackwell

Elizabeth Blackwell

(1821–1910)

Elizabeth Blackwell was the first modern woman to become a doctor. When she decided to become a physician, she was mocked, laughed at, treated as if she was insane, or simply ignored.

It took a very special person to overcome all this. Elizabeth Blackwell was just such a person.

Elizabeth was born on February 3, 1821, in Bristol, England, to Hannah and Samuel Blackwell. When she was born, she was so small that it was doubtful that she would survive.

Although Elizabeth never grew beyond five feet one inch in height, she possessed enough determination for someone twice her size.

Elizabeth's father, Samuel, a prosperous sugar refinery owner, was different from most men of his time. He insisted that his daughters be taught history, math, Latin, astronomy, and other subjects usually reserved for boys.

In 1832, when Elizabeth was eleven years old, the Blackwell family immigrated to America, seeking freedom from worker riots over better labor conditions. However, all they found in America was despair. Fire wiped out Samuel's sugar refinery in New York and left the family in dire financial straits.

In 1838, the Blackwells moved to Cincinnati, Ohio, to start over again. Samuel died suddenly in August, leaving his wife and six children nearly destitute.

The older children immediately got jobs. Elizabeth became a teacher. During one particularly desperate time, the once-prosperous family was so strapped for money that instead of buying fuel they all had to jump up and down in the parlor to keep warm.

The life of a schoolteacher for young women left Blackwell feeling empty and depressed. Trying to instruct girls who did not care about learning and only wanted to find husbands was not what she wanted to do with her life.

Then, early in 1845, an event occurred that changed everything for her.

One day Blackwell went to visit Mary Donaldson, a family friend who was dying of cancer.

As Blackwell was chatting away, Donaldson suddenly interrupted her. "You are fond of study, Elizabeth," she said. "You have health, leisure and a cultivated intelligence. Why don't you study medicine? Had I been treated by a lady doctor, my worst sufferings would have been spared me."[1]

The idea struck Blackwell as preposterous. There were no female physicians because medicine was a closed field to women. Blackwell found even the mention of the human body unpleasant. "The very thought of dwelling on the physical structure of the body and its various ailments filled me with disgust," she wrote in her journal that night.[2]

Yet the idea would not leave her. It was Blackwell's nature to attempt something difficult. Becoming a doctor would allow her to serve humanity—an idea that her father had always preached.

Finally, Blackwell thought that if she attempted this difficult career it would prevent her from getting married, which she felt would smother her intellectually.

So Elizabeth Blackwell decided to become a doctor. It would not be easy. Her friend Harriet Beecher Stowe, the writer, told her:

> You won't get into medical school. If you do, you won't have the money to pay for it. Not to mention the time—it takes years of study. Then afterwards, how will you get patients? People would never consult a woman doctor. Forget it. It can't be done.[3]

The more that Blackwell was told to forget it, the more determined she was to succeed.

Blackwell applied to all the medical schools in New York and Philadelphia, and was turned down by every one of them. Some people advised her to disguise herself as a man to gain admittance. Others said that only in Paris would she find a medical school to accept her, but that she shouldn't go there because the city was so sinful. "[I]f the path of duty leads me to hell I will go there," Blackwell said determinedly.[4]

Then, in October 1847, after applying to twenty-nine medical schools without success, Blackwell was accepted to the medical department of Geneva College in upstate New York.

The faculty at Geneva College, now Hobart College, had tried to avoid her controversial application by turning it over to the male students. The faculty told them that if they voted unanimously to accept Blackwell, then she could become a student.

The faculty never dreamed that the students would do precisely that. On November 7, 1847, Elizabeth Blackwell became student number 130 in the Geneva College Medical Department.

However, the people of Geneva refused to talk to her. They thought that she was either immoral, insane, or perhaps both. This worried Blackwell. She knew it was a preview of what was to come when she tried to establish her own medical practice.

Elizabeth Blackwell attended Geneva College in Geneva, N. Y. (shown here). Geneva was the only school that gave her a chance to attend their medical school. Geneva College is now known as Hobart College.

At school, however, it was a different matter. Although the term had begun four weeks earlier, Blackwell quickly caught up. She studied late into the night. To avoid blushing and seeming embarrassed during in-depth medical discussions, she starved herself so that her cheeks were extra pale.

When a friendly anatomy professor asked her to miss his lecture on reproduction that was famous for the use of frank terminology, Blackwell politely told him that she belonged there. She said that if her presence made him uncomfortable, she could sit in the back, without her bonnet.

When the professor told the other students of this conversation, he said that Blackwell had been right to insist on participating. The professor then opened the door to the classroom and Blackwell walked in, to thunderous applause.

After the school term ended in January 1848, Blackwell gained clinical experience by working at Blockley Almhouse in Philadelphia, which served as both a hospital and shelter for the poor.

She was assigned to the section for women with sexually-transmitted diseases such as syphilis, which causes body sores, insanity, and eventual death. As Blackwell watched her patients' pain and suffering, she became more determined that women, not men, should be in control of women's bodies and medical treatments.

Blackwell returned to Geneva College and finished her studies. On January 23, 1849, Elizabeth Blackwell graduated. The president of Geneva College, Dr. Benjamin Hale, left the awarding of Blackwell's diploma to the end.

An eyewitness wrote of that moment:

> She [Blackwell] ascended the steps. The President touched his cap and rose. You might have heard a pin drop. He . . . handed her the diploma and bowed. She seemed embarrassed and after an effort said . . . "I thank you kind Sir. It shall be the effort of my life, by God's blessing, to shed honor on this Diploma."[5]

Although she now had her medical degree, Blackwell found out that there was no hospital either in the United States or England that would let her practice medicine. In desperation she went to Paris and entered midwife training at La Maternité Hospital.

On November 4, 1849, while Blackwell was working at the hospital, some water that she was using to clean an infant's infected eye spurted into her own eye. Within hours, her left eye had swollen shut and the infection had spread to her other eye.

Her right eye recovered, but her left eye became blind. Eventually it had to be removed. With the loss of her left eye, Blackwell's dream of becoming a surgeon was no longer possible.

A lesser person might have sunk into despair, but Blackwell knew she could still practice medicine. After gaining clinical experience in London at St. Bartholomew's Hospital, Blackwell returned to America.

Once again she was rejected as a doctor by every major hospital in New York City. So Blackwell opened her own practice and waited for patients. They came—but very slowly.

In 1854, lonely and shunned by other members of her profession, Blackwell realized that she would never marry and have children. She decided to adopt a seven-year-old orphan named Katherine Barry, whom she called Kitty.

Other women were entering the medical field. In 1854, Blackwell's younger sister, Emily, became America's second female physician.

Elizabeth Blackwell continued to be an innovator. In 1857, she founded the New York Infirmary for Indigent Women and Children along with her sister, Emily, and a third female doctor, Marie Zakrzewska.

The following year Blackwell traveled to England, where she became the first woman to be listed in the British Medical Registry. In 1868, she and Emily founded the Woman's Medical College of the New York Infirmary.

The next year, with Emily coming into her own as a teacher and administrator, Elizabeth and Kitty moved permanently to England. Blackwell was forty-eight years old and was weary from a life spent fighting for her rights.

Blackwell opened a practice and taught at the London School for Medicine. However, by 1879, Blackwell's failing health forced her to retire to a country home in Hastings, England. Here, she wrote and campaigned vigorously for women's causes for the remainder of her life.

On May 31, 1910, Elizabeth Blackwell died at Hastings and was buried at Kilmun, Scotland. By then there were almost 7,400 women licensed as doctors in the United States.

The revolution begun by this small but determined woman had grown large indeed. Elizabeth Blackwell was truly a pioneer in medicine.

Clara Barton

(1821–1912)

At the age of thirty-two, Clara Barton was a young woman without a future. She was a single woman alone in the world, lacking any means of supporting herself.

By the time she died, Barton's name was synonymous with the American Red Cross, the organization she had founded. Clara Barton had gone from someone with no future to a person who had helped make the future brighter for millions of people.

Clarissa Harlowe Barton was born on Christmas Day, 1821, in North Oxford, Massachusetts, to Sara and Stephen Barton. She was their youngest child.

Clara Barton

Clara's brothers and sisters were so much older, Clara had no one her own age to talk to.

Clara grew up to be a quiet and painfully shy girl. As she later wrote: "[I]n the earlier years of my life I remember nothing but fear."[1] One place that Clara distinguished herself was in school. She was an exceptional student.

When Clara was eleven, her brother David, who she was very close to, was seriously injured helping to build a barn. Clara became his nurse and devoted two years of her life to caring for him.

Trying to conquer her extreme shyness, Clara decided to become a schoolteacher. On May 5, 1839, at age seventeen, Clara received her teaching certification and was given a teaching position in the North Oxford school district.

Despite her shyness, Clara became an extremely popular and effective teacher for more than a dozen years in the district.

Early in 1851, to further her knowledge, Barton enrolled at the Clinton Liberal Institute for female teachers in Clinton, New York. After graduating, Barton decided not to go back and teach in the North Oxford school district. She felt that opportunities for advancement there were limited.

Uncertain of what to do next, Barton went to visit her childhood friend, Mary Norton, in Hightstown, New Jersey.

In Hightstown, Barton took a job teaching at a "subscription" school where parents paid for their children to attend. But Barton was depressed and worried about her future. "I have grown weary of life," she wrote, "at an age when other people are enjoying it most."[2]

While on a visit to nearby Bordentown, New Jersey, Barton had noticed groups of children hanging about the streets. Their parents were too poor to pay for school and there was no free public education in New Jersey.

Barton decided to start a free school in Bordentown—possibly the first free public school in the state. Despite warnings about the terrible kinds of students who would attend her school, Barton won the support of local officials for her experimental school.

On the first day, six students showed up. By the end of the week there were forty students. After just one year, the number of students had reached a total of six hundred. A new school was built for them, but the Bordentown school board put a man in charge of the school instead of Barton.

Feeling betrayed and angry by this, Barton fell ill. To escape the stressful situation, she resigned her position and left Bordentown in February 1854, never to teach again.

From Bordentown, she went to Washington, D.C., to visit her sister. Barton worked for a short time as a clerk in the United States Patent Office. However, few women were working for the federal government then and male resentment toward Barton cost her this job.

Barton spent several aimless years back in North Oxford. In the spring of 1861, she returned to Washington, D.C. The administration of the new president, Abraham Lincoln, included a patent commissioner who had no objection to women working in his office.

On April 12, 1861, the American Civil War erupted between the Union and the Confederacy. Almost overnight the city of Washington was filled with soldiers who had responded to President Lincoln's call for volunteers. Among these was the 6th Massachusetts Regiment, which included men from Barton's home region, some of whom were her former students.

Upon hearing that the men had almost no provisions of any kind, Barton rushed out and bought as many useful things as she could. She hired men to help her transport everything to the 6th Massachusetts Regiment.

When Barton saw the gratitude in the soldiers' eyes, and realized how desperately needed her supplies were, she knew that she had found a sense of purpose to her life.

Immediately Barton launched a letter-writing campaign, urging friends and relatives to send supplies to her for the soldiers.

Private relief agencies around the country heard about what Barton was doing and sent her provisions.

Soon Barton had three warehouses packed to the ceiling with supplies and she began supplying hospitals with provisions as well.

Once the fighting started, Barton was dismayed to find that wounded Union soldiers were poorly cared for. Many died because the proper supplies were not on hand to treat them.

But bringing supplies was all Barton was allowed to do. Dorothea L. Dix, the champion of the mentally ill, had been appointed superintendent of nurses for the Union army. Dix did not want volunteer nurses such as Barton at the military hospitals where her professional nurses worked.

So Barton went out into the battlefields to help take care of the wounded there. At first Barton was uncertain whether it was proper for a single woman to go alone to the battlefields and army camps. But on his deathbed her father, a former soldier, told Barton: "I know soldiers, and they will respect you and your errand."[3] Then he told her to go and do whatever she could for the wounded.

Charged with her father's words, and with her own sense of patriotic duty, Barton began visiting Civil War battlefields to tend to the sick and wounded.

It was at the Battle of Antietam in September 1862, that Barton received the nickname by which she is still remembered today. Braving enemy shellfire, she brought linen, candles, and other needed items to the surgeons.

Dr. James Dunn, the surgeon in charge, nearly broke down in tears of relief when he saw Barton and her supplies. Later, describing all that Barton had done, he said, "[She is] the true heroine of the age, the angel of the battlefield."[4]

Barton spent the war at battlefields where it was so bad that sometimes she had to wring the blood from her skirt before she could stand and walk. Despite the emotions she felt while seeing all of the suffering, Barton did what she had to do.

Finally in April 1865, the Civil War ended. Barton, now famous, received President Lincoln's permission to look for missing soldiers. For nearly four years Barton tried to trace tens of thousands of soldiers whose lives had been swallowed up by the war. She succeeded in finding more than twenty-two thousand of these men.

When the Franco-Prussian War broke out in Europe in July 1870, Barton went to Geneva, Switzerland, to help nurse the wounded there. She learned about Jean-Henri Dunant, the Swiss phil-anthropist who had founded the Red Cross. Barton was astonished to see the efficiency with which the International Red Cross organized supplies and medicines received from all over Europe.

The directors of the International Red Cross were anxious for the United States to sign the 1864 Treaty of Geneva. By signing, the United States would be obligated to establish a branch of the Red

During the Civil War Battle of Antietam, Clara Barton braved enemy shellfire to bring supplies to surgeons. Here a surgeon is about to amputate a soldier's wounded leg.

Cross in America. But the United States did not want to sign a treaty devised by European countries.

Barton, however, inspired and moved by what she had seen in Europe, continued to press for the United States to sign the treaty and join the Red Cross. Even before the United States finally signed the treaty, Barton established the first branch of the American Red Cross in Dansville, New York, on August 22, 1881.

Then in the autumn of 1881, a terrible forest fire in northern Michigan left five thousand people homeless. Barton's new Red Cross organization rushed in to help. The U.S. officials were able to see firsthand the effect that the Red Cross had on people's lives during this disaster. They signed the Treaty of Geneva.

Barton's last years were unfortunately not good ones for her. She spent them fighting charges of impropriety and misuse of the funds of the organization she had founded. At the age of eighty-two, Barton lost control of the American Red Cross. But she left an organization that continues to help people everywhere.

When she died of pneumonia in 1912, Clara Barton was beloved around the world. The shy little girl from Massachusetts had made a big difference in the lives of people everywhere.

Mary Edwards Walker

Mary Edwards Walker
(1832–1919)

Mary Edwards Walker went through life always having to prove herself. She had to prove that she was as good a doctor as any man was. She had to prove that she deserved the Congressional Medal of Honor for her valiant service during the American Civil War.

Today, more than seventy-five years after her death, people are still arguing about this extraordinary woman's life. Even in death, it seems that Mary Edwards Walker still has to prove herself.

Mary Edwards Walker was born on November 26, 1832, on her family's farm in Oswego, New York. It was her father, Alvah, who exerted the most influence on Mary, her four sisters, and her brother.

In an age when most men favored keeping women in the home and not allowing them to attend school or go to work, Alvah Walker believed in education and employment equality for his daughters.

One women's equality issue that Mary's father was particularly adamant about was women's clothing. Women were expected to wear a dozen petticoats underneath a floor-length skirt and a tightly laced corset around their waist and upper body.

Mary's father endorsed the women's fashion revolution begun by Amelia Bloomer and her "bloomers"—a knee-length skirt worn over baggy trousers, which were gathered at the ankles. Mary shared her father's attitude toward women's clothing, and she fought her entire life to reform female fashion.

Her father also strongly influenced Mary in her decision to practice medicine. Besides running the family farm and teaching his children, Alvah Walker was a self-taught doctor.

Although Mary was raised to think that she could be anything she wanted to be, in reality her prospects of becoming a doctor were not good. Despite the example set by Elizabeth Blackwell, the first woman doctor of modern times, the medical profession in the 1850s was still virtually closed to women.

There were few medical schools that would accept women. At those schools that did, the environment was so hostile toward them that only the most determined females could survive. By 1858,

Mary Walker sometimes dressed in trousers to protest against the uncomfortable and restrictive clothes women were expected to wear.

only about three hundred women had graduated from medical schools in the United States, compared to eighteen thousand men.

But Mary Walker was not easily discouraged. By December 1853, she had saved enough money to enable her to enroll at Syracuse Medical College in Syracuse, New York. This was the first medical college in the United States, and it accepted both men and women equally.

Mary Walker graduated in June 1855. She was the only woman in her class. When she spoke at the graduation ceremony, she said, "As graduates, we are soon to leave and perform the active duties of the profession, and we trust you will never be pained by hearing that any have failed to be successful in, and respected by the community where we may chance to reside."[1]

Perhaps it was uncertainty of what she should do next that made her decide in 1856 to marry Dr. Albert Miller. She set up a practice with him in Rome, New York.

If Miller thought that marriage would make Walker conform to a more traditional role as wife and mother, he was sadly mistaken. On her wedding day, Walker wore pants and a man's coat instead of a wedding dress.

Miller's second shock came when his wife informed him that she would not be taking his name, as was the common practice then. She said that she would remain Mary Edwards Walker.

In 1859, both the marriage and the practice dissolved, although Walker and Miller were not officially divorced until 1869.

Walker never married again, but sometimes she felt the loss of companionship keenly. She once wrote: "[A true] conjugal companionship is the greatest blessing of which mortals can conceive in this life—to know that there is supreme interest in one individual, and that it is reciprocated."[2]

On April 12, 1861, the American Civil War began. Deeply patriotic, Walker journeyed to Washington, D.C. She felt that the urgent need for trained medical personnel would help her find validity as a doctor.

Walker's goal was to be appointed as a surgeon in the Union army, but she was turned down because she was a female. So she worked for two months as a volunteer assistant physician and surgeon.

Walker, unhappy that she had not received a commission, left Washington early in 1862, and went to New York City. After spending time with her family, she returned to Washington in the fall of 1862. She decided that the best way to prove her worth to Union medical officials was to demonstrate her skill out in the field.

Late in 1862, Walker traveled to Warrenton, Virginia, where the Union's Army of the Potomac was camped. Battered by recent engagements with the enemy and suffering from a typhoid fever epidemic, the Union army was in urgent need of qualified medical personnel.

Walker plunged into her duties—again as an unpaid volunteer—and quickly won the admiration of the Union army's commanding general, Ambrose Burnside.

In December 1862, the Union army suffered a terrible defeat at Fredericksburg, Virginia. Along with male field doctors, Walker again cared for the survivors, moving among "a carpet of bodies."[3]

She developed a reputation for not advocating amputation unless absolutely necessary. Most other field physicians often considered removal of an arm or leg as the best course of treatment for seriously damaged limbs.

Walker also became involved in women's rights activities. She helped to establish a residence for females who came to the city searching for wounded soldiers.

In late 1863, Walker again returned to the field after the Battle at Chickamauga. In spite of all that she had done as an unpaid volunteer, Walker's request for a commission was repeatedly denied by federal officials because she was a woman. In frustration, she sent an angry letter to President Abraham Lincoln in early January 1864.

Walker criticized a system that gladly used her services as a volunteer but refused to legitimize her by giving her a commission. In her letter, she said if a man had been as useful to the country as she had been, ". . . a star would have been taken from the National Heavens and placed upon his shoulder."[4]

Although Lincoln did not act on her behalf, Walker's luck was about to change.

Early in January 1864, the assistant surgeon of the 52nd Ohio Volunteers in the Union's Army of the Cumberland died suddenly. Union army commander George Thomas appointed Walker to the position as a civilian contract surgeon.

Besides tending to the men of the 52nd Ohio, Walker also went repeatedly into the surrounding Tennessee countryside outside of the Union lines to help the civilian population.

On April 10, 1864, Walker strayed too far from the Union camp and was captured by the Confederates. She spent the next four months as a southern prisoner of war in Richmond, Virginia. On August 12, 1864, Walker was exchanged for a captured Confederate major.

Walker's capture and imprisonment have raised questions as to whether or not she was a Union spy. General Thomas later thought that her appointment as a contract surgeon included an element of spying. When she wrote about her wartime experiences, Walker—never shy about talking about her activities—did not mention spying for the Union.

After the war ended in April 1865, Walker renewed her campaign for an army commission. President Andrew Johnson, who succeeded Abraham Lincoln after Lincoln was assassinated, was impressed by letters of support Walker received. But President Johnson was eventually persuaded not to grant her military employment because of doubts about her qualifications.

Still determined to recognize the wartime contributions of this extraordinary woman, Johnson signed a bill on November 11, 1865, that awarded Mary Edwards Walker the Congressional Medal of Honor. It was the first time in U.S. history that a woman had received this prestigious award.

During the time she spent in the Richmond prison, Walker's vision had been damaged and she no longer could practice medicine. To earn a living, she tried writing, lecturing, and even working as a clerk for the federal government. During the late 1880s and early 1890s, Walker was so destitute that she was even forced to lecture and exhibit herself at carnival sideshows to make money.

Walker continued working for women's causes, but her growing eccentricities—she usually dressed like a man—were more harmful than helpful to these groups. After a while she was not welcomed by them any longer.

In 1917, Walker's Medal of Honor, along with over nine hundred others, was revoked when Congress changed the requirements to include only actual combat with an enemy.

Although in her eighties by this time, the thin, frail Walker journeyed to Washington, D.C., once again. She defiantly announced that she would not return her medal and continued to wear it every day.

Walker's announcement was the last act of resistance from this fiery woman who had dedicated her whole life to fighting the establishment. On February 21, 1919, at the age of eighty-six, Mary Edwards Walker died at her home in Oswego.

In 1977, President Jimmy Carter reinstated her Medal of Honor. Mary Edwards Walker remains the first woman in the United States to have received this distinguished award for service to her country.

Susie King Taylor

Susie King Taylor
(1848–1912)

Susie King Taylor was a stranger in a strange land—an educated black woman during a time when that was an exception.

Susie served as washerwoman, teacher, and most importantly, nurse. She was one of the first African-American nurses in United States history. It is little wonder that we still celebrate the life of this remarkable woman today.

Susie Baker was born on August 6, 1848, into a world of slavery and poverty. Her mother, Hagar Ann Baker, was a slave on the Grest Farm on the Isle of Wight, one of a group of islands off the coast of South Carolina and Georgia.

Slave marriages were not legally recognized, and families were frequently split up. In 1855, at the age of seven, Susie, along with a brother, was sent to Savannah, Georgia, to live with their grandmother, Dolly Reed.

Once in Savannah, Susie and her brother were sent to their grandmother's friend, Mrs. Woodhouse, to learn how to read and write. Because it was illegal for blacks to be educated, Susie and her brother wrapped their books in paper to cover them and to keep white people or the police from seeing them.

Susie was an excellent student, learning everything that she could from her teachers. She even took secret lessons from some white friends as well.

On April 12, 1861, the American Civil War erupted between the Union and the Confederacy. Susie had been reading about people called Yankees. She had heard other blacks say how the Yankees were going to set the slaves free. "I wanted to see these wonderful 'Yankees' so much," Susie later wrote.[1]

In the early spring of 1862, the Union army attacked the Confederate-held Fort Pulaski at the mouth of the Savannah River. As the battle raged, slaves tried to flee to the coast, where they would be under the protection of the Yankees. Their white masters tried to stop them, and violence broke out everywhere.

On April 12, Fort Pulaski fell, leaving the Georgia countryside open to Union troops.

Frightened plantation owners fled with their families, leaving their slaves to fend for themselves.

Susie's uncle, along with other blacks, decided to try and reach St. Catherine's Island, which was held by the Union. Here, blacks were protected by the Yankee troops.

As the group of boats made their way toward the island, the Confederate boats fired on the ragtag fleet to try and stop them. One boat was sunk and another forced to turn back. Fortunately, Susie Baker's boat made it to safety.

Two weeks later Susie was placed on a Union gunboat for transfer to St. Simon's Island. Here her educated manner caught the attention of the ship's commander, Captain Whitmore.

Upon arrival at St. Simon's, the fourteen-year-old girl was put in charge of a school for former slaves. She taught both children and adults how to read and write.

Susie Baker and the rest of her group lived in constant fear. She later wrote:

> There were about six hundred men, women, and children on St. Simon's . . . and we were afraid to go very far from our own quarters in the daytime, and at night even to go out of the house for a long time. . . . The rebels . . . getting on the island would capture any persons venturing out alone and carry them to the mainland. Several of the men disappeared, and . . . were never heard from . . . [2]

But the men's valiant actions in pursuing the rebels rather than running had been noticed. In August 1862, many of the former slaves were sent to Beaufort, South Carolina, to help guard it and other areas that had been taken from the South by the North.

Because black soldiers weren't allowed in the Union army, the men formed their own volunteer regiment: the 1st South Carolina Volunteers. Susie Baker went along with them as their laundress, beginning her remarkable military career.

At Beaufort, Baker was kept busy washing the red coats and pants that the men in the regiment wore. She also taught lessons.

The men of the 1st South Carolina Volunteers were a fighting regiment. They soon found themselves in action against the Confederates. Their most important battle came in March 1863, when they captured the city of Jacksonville, Florida.

The fighting brought casualties, and soon the field hospitals were filled with wounded men. Medical care in the 1860s during the Civil War was extremely primitive. The cause of many infections was unknown. Doctors were poorly trained, and the usual remedy for a severe arm or leg wound was amputation.

Often the only comfort that could be given to a wounded soldier was for a nurse to change his bloody bandages and bathe his head with cool water. For this you did not need medical training, just

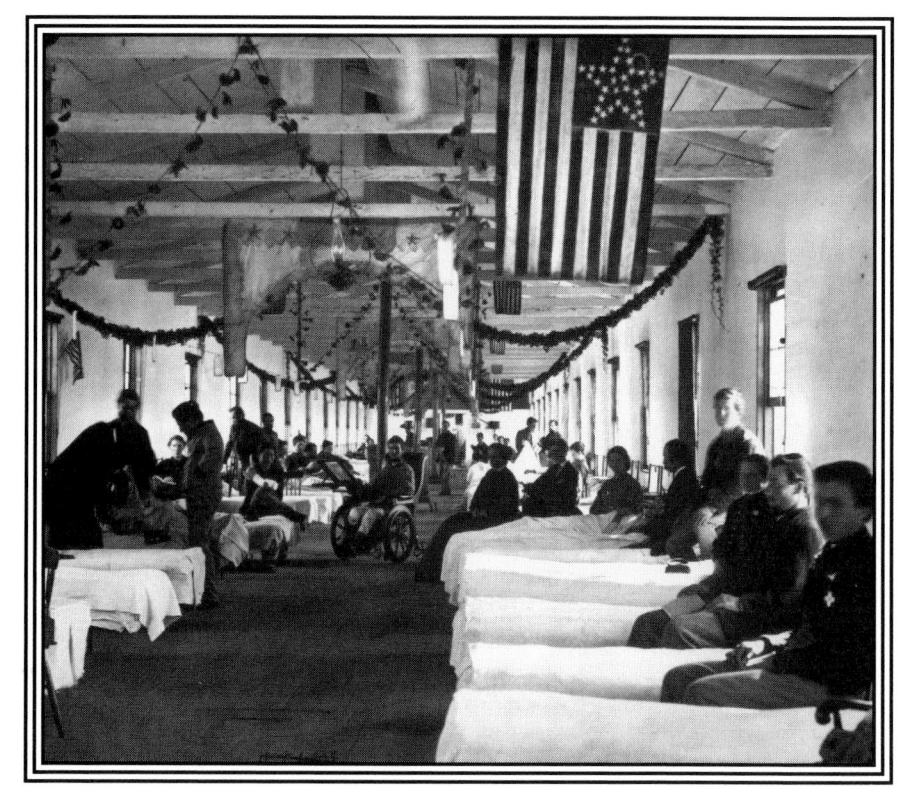

Susie King Taylor nursed patients at hospitals like this one during the American Civil War.

compassion, and young Susie Baker had this in abundance.

Baker began her career as a Civil War nurse by looking after several men who had contracted varioloid, a form of smallpox.

From that point on, Baker found herself spending more and more time at the hospital. Her unit, Company E, was repeatedly sent on

49

dangerous missions to destroy Confederate military fortifications and supply depots, and to free slaves.

The hospital began filling up with wounded men, and Baker was needed there almost constantly. She gave the soldiers medicine and changed their bloody bandages. She bathed them when they were feverish and helped them drink and eat when they could not do it for themselves.

Baker continued to live with the army in the field. She heated her small tent with hot coals taken from the cooking tent, just like the soldiers did. She ate the same sparse meals that the men ate, and she slept in the same flea-infested conditions as the rest of the army did.

But camp life was not all bad. It soon became apparent to Baker that Edward King, a sergeant with the 1st South Carolina Regiment, always seemed to have a wink and a smile for her. He seemed interested in being more than just friends. In 1863, fifteen-year-old Susie Baker and Edward King were married.

Susie Baker King was used to seeing things that would have terrified people twice her age. Going to a fort to watch the Union army shell Charleston, South Carolina, she had to pick her way through a field of human skulls. "They were a gruesome sight, those fleshless heads and grinning jaws, but by this time I had become accustomed to worse things . . ." she wrote.[3]

Indeed, she sometimes reflected on how the war had changed her, and all those who served with her.

> It seems strange how our aversion to seeing suffering is overcome in war, how we are able to see the most sickening sights, such as men with their limbs blown off and mangled by the deadly shells, without a shudder; and instead of turning away, how we hurry to assist in alleviating their pain . . .[4]

Susie King continued to do all that she could to help lessen the soldiers' pain, and her work did not go unnoticed.

One day at the Beaufort hospital, she met Clara Barton, one of the Civil War's most famous nurses, the woman who would later found the American Red Cross.

Susie King's nursing skill impressed Barton, and she often took King along whenever she visited the local hospitals.

Susie Baker King remained with the army until her regiment was mustered out in February 1866, following the end of the Civil War the previous year.

In 1866, Susie King became pregnant with her first child. Unfortunately, after all the suffering she had endured during the war, life had more hardships in store for her.

In 1866, her husband, Edward King, after having survived so many armed conflicts during the war, died of a head injury suffered in a fall. Susie King was left to bring up their baby alone.

Unable to teach, and denied entry into the nursing profession because of her race, Susie King worked as a cook, a maid, and a laundress to support herself and her baby.

In 1879, while living in Boston, she married Russell Taylor. Unfortunately he also died before she did, as did her only son.

However, Susie King Taylor carried on. She organized Corps 67, the Women's Relief Auxiliary, to help Union army veterans and their families. In 1902, she published her amazing book, *A Black Woman's Civil War Memoirs,* detailing her many experiences during the conflict.

Death came for Susie King Taylor on October 6, 1912, at the age of sixty-four. As she once wrote: "My dear friends! do we understand the meaning of war? . . . No, we do not. I can and shall never forget that terrible war until my eyes close in death."[5]

Today, thanks to her extraordinary contributions during the Civil War, the life of Susie King Taylor shall never be forgotten either.

Susan LaFlesche Picotte
(1865–1915)

Susan LaFlesche Picotte lived during a time of great change in the lives of her people, the Omaha Indians. The proud Omaha struggled to adjust to life on a reservation after living for generations on the Great Plains of the United States.

As the first American Indian woman to earn a medical degree, Susan LaFlesche Picotte became not just a doctor for the Omaha, but a beacon of hope for American Indians everywhere. Susan LaFlesche was born on June 17, 1865, the youngest daughter of Iron Eye, chief of the Omaha, and his wife, The One Woman. Besides Susan, the family consisted of four daughters and three sons.

Susan LaFlesche Picotte

Iron Eye's appointment as Omaha chief in 1853 had been controversial. Iron Eye was the son of an American Indian woman, who was either of the Ponca or Omaha tribe, and a French trader named Joseph LaFlesche. Iron Eye—whose English name was also Joseph LaFlesche—knew that when he looked into the future, he saw the traditional way of life of the Plains Indians fast disappearing.

While other chiefs were angry about losing their culture, Iron Eye accepted it stoically. He felt that the best thing to do was to prepare his people and the people of other tribes to live in the white world.

Because Iron Eye felt so strongly about assimilating the Omaha into the white world, he did not give either Susan or her sisters the Indian markings that symbolized they were daughters of a chief.

He sent his children to the reservation's white school, and he called himself and his children by their white names. He had the Omaha learn English.

Yet even as he urged his people to learn the white culture, Iron Eye fought fiercely for the rights of the Omaha and the other American Indian tribes.

In the fall of 1879, fourteen-year-old Susan and her sister Marguerite were sent to attend the Elizabeth Institute for Young Ladies in Elizabeth, New Jersey. Here Susan learned philosophy, physiology, and literature, as well as about the white culture.

When she returned to the reservation in 1882, Susan was uncertain about the direction of her life.

One subject that had interested her since she was young was medicine.

Then, in 1883, Susan helped nurse back to health a white woman, Alice Fletcher. Fletcher, who was studying the Omaha culture, had developed a severe case of rheumatism. That experience struck a responsive chord inside Susan.

But perhaps the main reason that Susan decided to become a doctor was her desire to help the Omaha.

After years of living out in the open air and in teepees on the Great Plains, the Omaha were now struggling to adapt to living in wooden homes on the reservation. Many Omaha became ill from living in such closed-up, cramped quarters, and the white doctors were of little or no help.

Susan reasoned that if her people were expected to live like whites, then they deserved the same quality of medical care. Perhaps, as a doctor, she could help bring good medical treatment and care to the Omaha and other American Indians.

Susan knew that the road to becoming the first female American Indian physician would not be easy, but she had an iron determination to succeed.

She attended Hampton Normal and Agricultural Institute in Virginia with two of her sisters. Susan worked hard and studied intently.

As the second best student in her class, Susan was given the honor of addressing the audience at the graduation ceremonies in May 1886. In her speech, she said, "The shores of success can only be reached by crossing the bridge of faith, and I shall try hard."[1]

Those were not just empty words for Susan. Just before graduation she learned that she had been accepted at the Women's Medical College in Philadelphia.

Many people were counting on her to succeed, including the women of the Connecticut Indian Association, who were paying her tuition. Above all, Susan LaFlesche carried the hopes of the entire Omaha tribe on her shoulders.

As Iron Eye had told her: "Learn all that they can teach you . . . and say, 'I owe this doctor wisdom to the Omaha.'"[2] LaFlesche knew that only by trying very hard indeed would she not let everyone down.

LaFlesche entered the Women's Medical College in October 1886. Although the courses were hard—students had to maintain an academic average of 90 or above—she always found time to write letters home.

On March 14, 1889, Susan LaFlesche graduated among the top students in her class at the Women's Medical College. Sadly, her father did not live to see her triumph. He had died the previous fall.

Late in 1889, LaFlesche returned to the Omaha reservation. Although she began as the physician for the agency school in May, she was quickly appointed by the government to be the doctor for the entire Omaha tribe—1,244 people.

With so many people in her care, LaFlesche found herself constantly traveling around the reservation, first on horseback, and later in a covered wagon.

LaFlesche traveled across the Nebraska plains no matter what the weather. In the summer the merciless heat baked her skin, and in the winter the frigid wind drove tiny grains of sand into her eyes, making it difficult to see. Rain soaked her clothing until the dampness seemed to settle in her bones. Snow froze her skin, but nothing stopped LaFlesche from delivering her care, her medicine, and her wisdom.

However, in her fervent desire to help the sick, Susan LaFlesche neglected her own health. After four years the bones in her face ached from constant exposure to harsh weather. She suffered from headaches, earaches, and backaches.

Although she was only twenty-eight years old, LaFlesche was exhausted. It was with a heavy heart that she resigned as the government doctor in October 1893.

In 1894, LaFlesche, who had always assumed that she would never wed because of the tremendous demands of her profession, surprised everyone by marrying Henry Picotte. He was a Sioux Indian who performed in a Wild West show.

The couple moved to Bancroft, Nebraska, in the southern part of the Omaha reservation. Soon Susan LaFlesche Picotte felt well enough to begin practicing medicine again. Along with her husband and

This is the home Susan LaFlesche Picotte shared with her husband, Henry, and their two children, Carl and Pierre.

their two children, Carl and Pierre, she enjoyed several years of happiness.

She was not only a doctor for the Omaha, but she was a teacher as well. She stressed the importance of proper sanitation and the need to keep flies and other insects out of homes.

She also strongly warned about the evils of alcoholism, which was taking a terrible toll not only on the Omaha but also on other American Indian tribes. Susan Picotte waged a vigorous campaign against alcoholism—a campaign that took on added personal significance when the disease claimed her husband in 1905.

Although Susan Picotte suffered repeated relapses of facial pain, earaches, and other ailments, she continued working tirelessly on behalf of her people and all American Indians.

In 1905, Picotte was appointed as a Presbyterian missionary to the Omaha tribe—the first American Indian ever given that position.

Five years later, even though she was even sicker than before, and had suffered a drastic loss of hearing, she went to Washington, D.C. There, she successfully lobbied the federal government for the rights of the Omaha to manage the money that they were to receive from the sale of their lands.

Picotte's greatest victory, however, came on January 8, 1913, when Walthill Hospital in Walthill, Nebraska, opened. It was the first hospital on the Omaha reservation—a hospital made possible only by the relentless dedication and effort of "Dr. Sue."

By that time, however, the bright light that was Susan LaFlesche Picotte was beginning to fade. Years of illness and hard work had taken their toll on the Omaha woman.

In the spring of 1915, she had two operations on the bones of her face, but the operations were unsuccessful. On September 18, 1915, she died at the age of fifty.

At the end of her funeral service, which was conducted by three clergymen, the final prayer was spoken in the ancient Omaha language of Umonhon. Even in death, Susan LaFlesche Picotte was still comfortable in both the white and the American Indian worlds.

Clara Maass
(1876–1901)

Today there are few people who know the name Clara Maass. No one speaks of her as they do other famous women of medicine, even though there is a hospital named in her honor in New Jersey.

At the beginning of the twentieth century, however, many people in the United States knew the name Clara Maass. She was a national hero, a brave young woman who gave her life to help defeat yellow fever, a terrible disease.

Clara Louise Maass was born in East Orange, New Jersey, on June 28, 1876. She was the oldest of nine children of Robert E. and Hedwig Maass, who had come to the United States from Germany.

Nurse Clara Louise Maass, U.S.A.
Yellow Fever Heroine. Class of 1895, Lutheran
Memorial Hospital, now Clara Maass Memorial

Clara Maass

While still in elementary school, Clara took a job with a family helping the mother take care of her children and her home. At an age when most other children were playing and enjoying themselves, Clara had grown-up responsibilities.

When Clara was fifteen, she left East Orange High School, after completing just three years, to take a full-time job working with children in the Newark Orphan Asylum.

The following year, Clara enrolled in the nursing school of Newark German Hospital in Newark, New Jersey. Although the hospital wanted women between the ages of twenty and forty for its nurses' training program, Clara looked and acted much older than her real age of sixteen.

When Anna Seeber, the head nurse at Newark German hospital at the time, interviewed Clara for entrance into the program, Seeber could tell that Clara would be able to take the hard work and long hours of nursing.

For the next two years Clara worked tirelessly at being a nurse. The work was difficult; of six women who had started the program the year before, only one woman had graduated.

But Clara persevered. On October 12, 1895, she and three others received their nursing cap and pin from Newark German Hospital. Clara worked hard at her job, and in 1898, became the head nurse at the hospital. Clara Maass seemed set to embark on a long career as a nurse, when her life took an unexpected turn.

On February 15, 1898, the United States battleship *Maine,* anchored in the harbor at Havana, Cuba, exploded and 266 sailors died. Two months later the United States was at war with Spain, which controlled Cuba.

The Spanish-American War lasted less than four months, with the United States victorious. As a result, the United States gained control of Guam, Puerto Rico, and the Philippine Islands from Spain.

Spanish soldiers, however, were not the only enemies the Americans had to fight in Cuba; there were also diseases, including yellow fever.

Yellow fever is a highly contagious disease. When the disease struck a port city, a yellow quarantine flag was flown, alerting incoming ships to avoid the port at all costs.

The Spanish called the disease *el vomito negro,* which means "the black vomit," because of the dark color caused by internal bleeding. The name "yellow fever" comes from two of the symptoms: a high fever and a jaundiced or yellow skin caused by the disease. Since medical science did not know what caused yellow fever, there was no cure.

When the Spanish-American War began, Maass applied to become a "contract nurse." This meant that she would be paid by the United States Army to care for sick and wounded soldiers.

But by the time she received her assignment, the brief war was over. On February 5, 1899, Maass's contract with the army expired, and she returned to work at Newark German Hospital.

When American troops were sent to the Philippine Islands to quell a rebellion there, Maass again volunteered her services. "I am in excellent health and I have a good constitution, and am accustomed to the hardships of field service,"[1] she wrote.

On November 20, 1899, Maass was sent to Manila, the capital of the Philippines. When she arrived, the city was in the midst of a massive yellow-fever epidemic.

For seven months Maass nursed the sick soldiers. Then she was stricken with dengue fever, an illness that causes great pain in the joints and muscles. The army sent her home in the summer of 1900 to recover.

Encouraged by the news that the *Anopheles* mosquito had been identified as the carrier of malaria, scientists and doctors wondered if an insect might also cause yellow fever.

In the summer of 1900, several physicians met in Cuba determined to find the cause of yellow fever. Led by an American doctor, Walter Reed, the group targeted the *Aedes aegypti* mosquito as a likely carrier of the disease.

Meanwhile, the city of Havana, Cuba, was in the grip of another yellow-fever epidemic. Dr. William Gorgas, who was in charge of sanitation for the United States Army, issued an urgent call for nurses to help Havana's sick, and Maass went to help.

When she arrived in Cuba in November 1900, Maass was assigned to Las Animas Hospital, a civilian hospital in Havana. Here she learned from Dr. Juan Guiteras, the Havana health officer, about the yellow-fever research underway.

As part of the study, Dr. Guiteras was attempting to immunize people against the disease by inoculating volunteers with a mild case of yellow fever from infected mosquitoes.

In the late spring of 1901, desperate for test subjects, the United States Army offered one hundred dollars to anyone who volunteered to be bitten by an infected mosquito.

Six Spanish immigrants volunteered for the test. Two of them died. In June 1901, Maass volunteered for the experiment. Perhaps Maass hoped that the experiment would give her immunity to yellow fever. She was the only woman to volunteer.

In a letter to her mother, Maass said she was sending home one hundred dollars to help pay bills. She also told her mother that part of the one hundred dollars could pay the way for her sister Sophia to come to Cuba.

On June 24, 1901, Clara Maass bared her arm to a mosquito suspected of carrying yellow fever. Although she caught the illness, it was a mild case, and she quickly recovered.

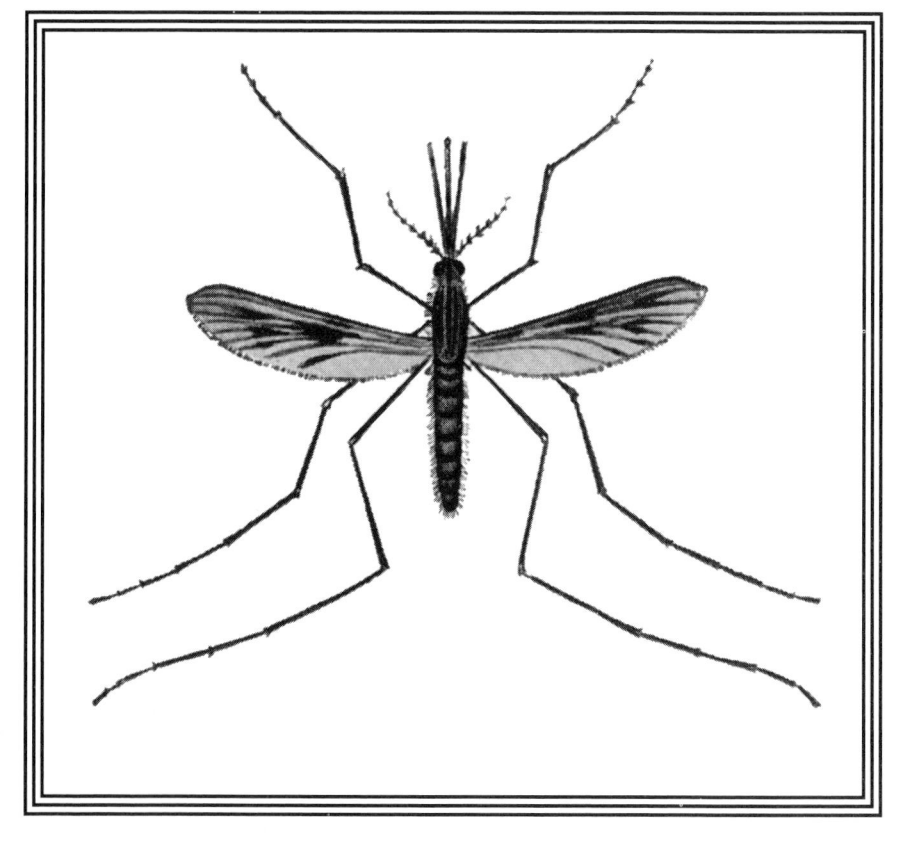

Clara Maass volunteered to be bitten by a mosquito like this one in an experiment to help find a cure for yellow fever. The mosquito shown here is the *Anopheles quadrimaculatus* mosquito.

Dr. Guiteras and his fellow physicians, however, did not feel that the weak case of yellow fever had truly immunized Maass against the disease. So on August 14, Maass submitted to the test again.

This time, however, she contracted a severe case of yellow fever. Although desperately ill, Maass managed to write a last letter home. "Good-bye, Mother," it said. "Don't worry, God will care for me . . . You know I am the man of the family but do pray for me."[2]

On August 20, a telegram from Dr. Gorgas arrived at the Maass home in New Jersey saying that Clara Maass had yellow fever.

Sophia immediately took a ship to Havana. While she was en route, her mother received another telegram from Dr. Gorgas dated August 24: "Miss Maass worse."[3]

On August 25, 1901, came the final telegram from Dr. Gorgas stating Maass had died the day before.

Sophia had arrived in Havana shortly before her sister's death. After burying her sister in Havana's Colon Cemetery, Sophia sailed for home, taking Clara Maass's few belongings with her. Clara Maass was the only woman and the only American to die during the yellow fever experiments of 1900–01.[4]

Her death ended the yellow-fever experiments. Although they caused some controversy over the use of humans as experimental subjects, her death proved that immunity could not be obtained in that way. It also removed any doubts concerning the *Aedes aegypti* mosquito as the disease carrier.

Dr. Gorgas began a swift and systematic extermination program of the insect. His success was nothing short of spectacular. There was not a single case of yellow fever reported in Havana from

October 1901, to June of the following year as a result of his efforts.

Maass's death was front-page news in the *New York Journal* of August 25, 1901. The *New York Times* carried an editorial praising her courage: "No soldier in the late war placed his life in peril for better reasons than those which prompted this faithful nurse to risk hers."[5]

In gratitude, the United States Army sent Maass's casket home to be buried in Newark's Fairmount Cemetery.

In 1952, the former Newark German Hospital was renamed Clara Maass Hospital in her honor. In 1976, the United States issued a thirteen-cent stamp with Maass's picture to commemorate the one hundredth anniversary of her birth. (Twenty-five years earlier, in 1951, Cuba had issued a two-cent stamp honoring her.)

What made the American honor significant was that it took place during the nation's bicentennial year, when there were dozens of much more famous heroes to choose from.

Thanks to Clara Maass, a terrible disease, which had plagued civilization for centuries, was finally conquered. Clara Maass was—and always will be—a hero for all time.

Gertrude Radnitz Cori

Gerty Radnitz Cori

(1896–1957)

As a child, Gerty Theresa Radnitz was taught to appreciate the finer things in life, such as music, ballet, and the theater. Later, she attended a special school to learn social skills. All of this was supposed to help Gerty attract a good husband.

In the European world of the late nineteenth century, the period in which Gerty lived, finding a husband was considered the most important thing that a woman could accomplish in life.

But Gerty Radnitz was ambitious. She wanted to do great things as well. Her ambition led her to become a pioneering biochemist and, ultimately, the first American woman to win a Nobel Prize in science.

Gerty Theresa Radnitz was born on August 15, 1896, in Prague, in what is now the Czech Republic. She was the oldest of three girls born to Otto and Martha Radnitz. Gerty's father was a successful chemist who managed sugar refineries.

For the first ten years of her life Gerty was educated privately at home by a special tutor. She was then sent to a girls' lyceum, a type of finishing school designed to complete a woman's education by teaching her social skills and culture.

Gerty's Uncle Robert, a professor of pediatrics at Carl Ferdinand University in Prague, felt that Gerty could do more with her life than just become a social accessory to a husband. He encouraged Gerty to study mathematics and science.

Inspired by her uncle, Gerty at age sixteen decided she wanted to study medicine at Carl Ferdinand University, which had recently dropped its ban against female students.

However, Gerty did not have the strong academic background necessary to enter the university. She discovered that she would need the equivalent of eight years of Latin, five years of math, and some chemistry and physics in order to pass the entrance exam.

Soon after this, Gerty and her family went on a vacation to the Austrian Alps. There, she met a high-school teacher and she asked him to teach her Latin. Gerty proved to be an excellent pupil. By the end of her vacation, she had learned three years of Latin.

When she returned home, Gerty enrolled in the Realgymnasium at Tetschen, a school that taught the necessary academic subjects for students who would be entering college. Incredibly, Gerty mastered all of the subjects that she needed in one year.

In 1914, at eighteen, Gerty took the entrance exams for Carl Ferdinand University. They were, she later said, "the hardest examinations I was ever called upon to take."[1] She passed the exams and was enrolled in the university's medical school.

Gerty had gone to college to find a career. She did not expect to also find love there. In an anatomy class during her first semester at school, Gerty met a student named Carl Cori. They quickly discovered that they had similar interests, and both knew that they wanted to become medical researchers rather than physicians.

They studied together throughout medical school. In 1920, they graduated and made plans to marry. However, Carl's family opposed the marriage because he was Roman Catholic and Gerty was Jewish.

Anti-Semitism (prejudice of Jews) was sweeping through Europe. The Cori family was afraid that if their son married a Jew it would hurt his career. Gerty agreed to convert to Catholicism so that the marriage could take place.

After they were married, the couple moved to Vienna, Austria, where both hoped to find opportunities as medical researchers. But Europe's economy was still recovering from the impact of World War I. There were few jobs of any kind available.

For a time Gerty Cori worked at the Carolinen Children's Hospital in Vienna, while her husband took a job in the pharmacology department at the University of Graz. Finally, they both realized that if they truly wanted to pursue careers as medical researchers, they would have to leave Europe.

In 1922, Carl Cori left for the United States and took a job at the New York State Institute for the Study of Malignant Diseases in Buffalo, New York. Gerty Cori stayed behind in Vienna. Six months later she got a job at the same place as her husband.

Initially, the Coris studied cancerous tumors and how they grew by using sugar for energy. But they were also interested in insulin, a hormone in the human body that had been discovered in 1921. Insulin played an important part in controlling the amount of sugar in the blood of people with diabetes.

Gerty Cori had been interested in sugar metabolism and diabetes ever since her father, who was a diabetic, said to her: "You're a doctor now. Why don't you find a cure for diabetes?"[2]

The couple decided to focus their research on the chemical process of carbohydrate metabolism, which is how tissues in the human body store and use sugar.

To discover what they wanted to know, the Coris fed sugar to laboratory rats. Then they examined what happened to the sugar if they fed the rats insulin.

They found that sugar enters the bloodstream in a form called glucose. The body burns some for energy, some is converted to fat, and the remainder is converted to a carbohydrate called glycogen. The glycogen is stored in the liver and the muscles. When they fed insulin to the rats, it decreased the amount of sugar stored in the liver.

What the Coris discovered was that the body utilized sugar in a continuous cycle. This cycle became known as the Cori cycle.

They found that glycogen breaks down into glucose, which is a form that the muscles can use for energy. When the muscles use glucose for energy, the glucose leaves a residue of lactic acid. The lactic acid travels through the bloodstream to the liver, where it is converted back to glucose. The glucose is then brought back to the muscles, where it is once again converted to glycogen and stored until needed for energy. Then the whole cycle begins again.

This was a revolutionary discovery by the Coris, who worked together as a true team. Gerty took the lead role in the laboratory as often as Carl did. The couple worked together so seamlessly that a newspaper declared that "it is hard to tell where the work of one leaves off and that of the other begins."[3]

In 1931, the Coris went to work for Washington University in St. Louis, Missouri. Carl Cori became a professor of pharmacology and biochemistry and Gerty Cori accepted a secondary position as a research fellow in pharmacology.

Gertrude Radnitz Cori worked closely with her husband, Carl F.
Cori (shown here). Together they founded the model for the "Cori
cycle," a blueprint of how the body stores and uses sugar.

In 1936, Gerty Cori gave birth to a son, Thomas. By then she had begun studying enzymes (special proteins that allow chemical reactions to occur in living organisms), about which little was known.

Thanks to the Coris' research, new enzymes were found, as well as a new form of glucose that today is called Cori ester in their honor.

In 1939, they discovered the enzyme that was responsible for converting glycogen to glucose and then reversing the process.

These discoveries by the Coris were critically important in a number of medical areas, including understanding how diabetes works. Their discoveries were important as well to a number of illnesses that are caused by missing enzymes.

Thanks to her brilliant work, Gerty Cori finally began to overcome some of the sexual bias that had barred her from receiving the recognition she deserved.

The biggest honor for Gerty Cori came in 1947, when she and her husband as a team shared the Nobel Prize for Physiology or Medicine with Argentine physiologist Bernardo A. Houssay. The Coris received their Nobel Prize for the research they did in enzymes and the discovery of the Cori cycle. This made Gerty Cori the first American woman, and the third female worldwide, to win a Nobel Prize in the sciences.

"Our efforts have been largely complementary, and one without the other would not have gone as far as in combination," said Carl when he accepted his award.[4]

But if the year 1947 held happiness for Gerty, it held sorrow for her as well. During a mountain-climbing expedition that year she fainted. A medical examination revealed that she was suffering from myelosclerosis, a rare and fatal illness caused by the destruction of bone marrow.

For the last ten years of her life Gerty waged a valiant battle against her illness. Sometimes she became discouraged, saying once to a coworker, "If something like this happens to you, it's better that a ton of bricks should fall on you."[5]

But Gerty refused to let her illness interfere with her research. "The love for and dedication to one's work seems to me to be the basis for happiness," she once said.[6] Even as her condition worsened, she continued working in her laboratory on her research.

She said, "For a research worker the unforgotten moments of . . . life are those rare ones, which come after years of plodding work, when the veil over nature's secret seems suddenly to lift and when what was dark and chaotic appears in a beautiful light and pattern."[7]

When she died on October 26, 1957, at the age of sixty-one, Gerty Radnitz Cori had lifted the veil on so many of nature's secrets that the light she revealed illuminated the entire world.

Antonia Coello Novello
(1944–   )

When Antonia Novello was a young girl in Puerto Rico, she was so sick that she would have to spend part of every summer in a hospital for treatment. These bouts of illness inspired her to become a doctor so she could help others, particularly children, so they would not suffer as she did.

Not only did Novello ultimately become a doctor, but she was appointed to be the surgeon general of the United States—the first Hispanic and the first woman to ever hold that office.

Antonia Coello was born on August 23, 1944, in Fajardo, Puerto Rico. Her parents, Antonio and Ana Delia Flores Coello, divorced when Antonia was very

Antonia Coello Novello

young. Her father died by the time Antonia reached her fourth birthday, so she didn't really get a chance to know him. Eventually her mother, a teacher who later became a principal at Yabucoa High School in Puerto Rico, remarried.

Most of the people who lived in Fajardo worked on farms. They were poor, and often did not have the money to pay for proper medical care. As a result, many of their children were frequently sick.

Antonia was not a healthy child either. She had been born with a chronic illness of the colon, which is a part of the large intestine. Sometimes her colon would swell, causing Antonia both discomfort and pain. This condition was so bad that every summer she would have to go to a hospital for several weeks. There the doctors would treat her until she became well enough to return home.

As a result of her illness, Antonia decided that she would like to devote her life to helping other sick children by becoming a doctor. But becoming a doctor was a difficult thing to do for a young girl from Fajardo without much money.

"All I wanted to do when I dreamed was to become a pediatrician, a doctor for the little kids in my hometown," she said later. "I never told anyone that I wanted to be that. It seemed too grand of a notion."[1]

Antonia knew that the best way for her to attain her dream was to study hard in school. Her high school grades were so good that she received a scholarship to the University of Puerto Rico in Rio Piedras.

Here Antonia studied biology. She graduated in 1965 with a bachelor of science degree. That same year she was accepted as a student at the university's medical school, and began studying to become a doctor.

Studying to be a doctor is not easy. In addition to the difficult course work, Antonia was faced with two very stressful events in her first year as a medical student. The first was when her aunt died because doctors did not know how to treat her aunt's failing kidneys.

The second event was a serious reoccurrence of her colon condition. Although Antonia had had an operation when she was eighteen to correct the condition, it had been only partially successful. Now the problem flared up again. She became extremely ill and had to have a second operation. Fortunately, this time the problem was corrected.

However, it was not all studying and stress for Antonia in medical school. While she was a student there, she met Joseph Novello, a U.S. Navy flight surgeon. The two fell in love, and were married the day after Antonia graduated from medical school in 1970.

The newlyweds moved to Ann Arbor, Michigan, to continue their medical education. Antonia Novello worked as an intern in the pediatric nephrology unit at the University of Michigan Medical Center. This unit specialized in treating children with kidney disease.

Antonia Novello worked very hard and had such an understanding of the problems these children were going through that she was named Intern of the Year. It was the first time that a woman had ever received this award from the medical center's pediatric department.

When Antonia Novello decided that she was ready to open her own medical practice, she and her husband moved to Washington, D.C. There she opened a pediatric practice and began treating children. But after just two years, she gave it up because she became too close to the children she was treating, and couldn't stand to watch them suffer with illness.

Novello continued her medical education, earning a master's degree in public health from Johns Hopkins University in 1982. Four years later she became deputy director of the National Institute of Child Health and Human Development. Here she took particular interest in children with acquired immune deficiency syndrome (AIDS).

Besides AIDS, Novello also became an expert on many other health and medical issues. From 1978 to 1990, Novello worked for the U.S. Public Health Service. During those twelve years, she tried to focus attention on issues of concern to the public, such as organ transplants and substance abuse among teenagers.

Her work and distinguished reputation caught the attention of President George Bush. In the fall of 1989, Bush nominated Antonia Novello to become the surgeon general of the United States. The surgeon general's job is to keep the public informed about important medical issues such as information about AIDS and the relationship between smoking and lung cancer.

On March 9, 1990, Antonia Novello was sworn in as the U.S. surgeon general. She was the first Hispanic and the first female to hold that high office.

In her remarks on the day she was sworn in, Novello paid tribute to the dreams she had had as a young child. "Somewhere this very morning, anywhere in San Francisco, San Antonio, Boston, Biloxi, there's another minority girl or boy who can dream the dreams that I just dreamed yesterday of becoming the Surgeon General of this country."[2]

When Novello returned to her hometown in Puerto Rico for her first public appearance as surgeon general, she said, "I realized that for these people, for women, I have to be good as a doctor, I have to be good as a Surgeon General, I have to be everything,"[3]

In the speech that she made when she was sworn in, Antonia Novello said that her motto as the surgeon general would be "good science and good sense."

She worked to heighten awareness of how pregnant women with AIDS can transfer the virus that causes the illness to their children. "AIDS is the only epidemic in the world where children will survive their parents," she said. "We've got to do the best we can for all children."[4]

Antonia Novello became the first Hispanic Surgeon General of the United States. She was appointed by former President George Bush.

As part of her good sense approach, Novello highlighted the dangers of cigarette smoking and alcohol and, in particular, the effects of both on children. She waged a vigorous campaign to stop advertisements targeted at young people that portrayed cigarette smoking and drinking as cool.

Novello also tried to focus attention on the health problems of Hispanic/Latino Americans. She publicized facts about them that many people did not know, such as how more Hispanic Americans have kidney disease than do other American ethnic groups.

By the time her term as the U.S. surgeon general ended in 1993, Antonia Novello had become a familiar figure to most Americans.

As the surgeon general, Novello had waged a constant and determined campaign to focus attention on underage drinking and smoking, AIDS, domestic violence, and the health problems of minorities. She worked hard to develop national awareness and concern about these and other health issues facing the people of the United States.[5]

After serving her term as U.S. Surgeon General, Novello was appointed to serve as New York State Health Commissioner in 1999. She is currently in charge of one of the leading health agencies in the nation and manages a budget of more than $27 billion dollars.

During her time as surgeon general and in her current role as health commissioner, Novello has played a major role in health programs and legislation. The impact of her work can especially be seen in initiatives she developed for disenfranchised groups such as women, children, and minorities.

Novello's continuing efforts are apparent today as she addresses major health issues affecting the people of New York State such as affordable healthcare and AIDS. Her actions to improve the health of Americans have proved that Antonia Novello is indeed a woman of her word.

Mae Carol Jemison

Mae Carol Jemison
(1956–   )

Adults often tell children to "reach for the stars." They mean by this to encourage children to try and achieve as much as they possibly can in their life. No goal is too high to try and obtain.

Mae Jemison took this advice literally. Not only did Jemison reach for the stars—she grabbed hold of them.

When Mae Carol Jemison was born on October 17, 1956, in Decatur, Alabama, the U.S. government program that would eventually take her to the stars did not yet exist. This was the National Aeronautics and Space Administration (NASA), which was a program established two years later under a law signed by President Dwight Eisenhower.

When Mae was three years old her parents—Charlie, a carpenter and roofer, and Dorothy, an elementary school teacher—moved their family, to Chicago. This is where Mae and her brother and sister grew up.

In the early 1960s, NASA and the American space program began a series of manned space flights, with the object of putting a man on the moon by the end of the decade. Mae, who had developed an early interest in science and astronomy, followed these flights with fascination.

In July 1969, man stepped foot on the moon for the very first time when American astronauts Neil Armstrong and Edwin "Buzz" Aldrin walked on the lunar surface. This historic event fueled twelve-year-old Mae's interest in science even further.

Medicine proved to be just as powerful a lure to Mae as space travel was. She worked in the laboratory at a local hospital and researched sickle-cell anemia, a disease that primarily affects African Americans.

After graduating from high school, Mae attended Stanford University in California, where she majored in chemical engineering and African-American studies.

Scientist, astronaut, doctor—these were not typical careers for a young African-American woman to seek during the early 1970s. Although professions like these were just opening up to minorities at this time, it was mainly males who were entering them. But nothing was going to stop Mae Jemison from pursuing her dreams.

After graduating from Stanford University in 1977 with degrees in both chemical engineering and African-American studies, Jemison began the pursuit of another goal. She enrolled in Cornell University Medical College to study medicine.

In 1981, Mae Jemison graduated from Cornell with a medical degree. The following year she went to work as a doctor in Los Angeles. But Jemison was not the type to sit in an office and see patients.

Jemison knew that there were many people in other parts of the world who could use her help. So in January 1983, at the age of twenty-six, she joined the Peace Corps, an American agency that helps people in underdeveloped countries.

For two and a half years, Jemison worked for the Peace Corps. She was the area medical officer for the West African nations of Sierra Leone and Liberia. She supervised the medical staff, worked on public medical care, taught volunteer personnel, and wrote medical manuals. Jemison also developed and participated in research projects on diseases such as hepatitis B and rabies.

Upon her return to the United States in mid-1985, Jemison resumed working, serving as a general practitioner in Los Angeles. But she had not forgotten her lifelong dream of traveling to the stars, and now it seemed as if this dream was closer than ever.

NASA had begun recruiting more women, minority pilots, and mission specialists for its space-shuttle program. Mae decided that the time was right for her to pursue yet another of her goals. In October 1985, she applied for admission to NASA's astronaut-training program.

Then disaster struck. On January 28, 1986, the space shuttle *Challenger* exploded as it was hurtling through earth's atmosphere to reach outer space. All seven astronauts aboard were killed. The astronaut selection program and he space-shuttle flight schedule were suspended as NASA tried to determine what had gone so terribly wrong.

It would be more than two years until the space shuttle flew again. But the astronaut-training selection program began again in October 1986. Jemison again submitted her name; the *Challenger* disaster had not discouraged her from pursuing her dream.

One of the reasons that Jemison still wanted to participate in the space program was her belief that outer space is one of the keys to the future of life on earth. She says that space "is the birthright of everyone who is on this planet. We need to get every group of people in the world involved because it is something that eventually we in the world community are going to have to share."[1]

In February 1987, Jemison received word that she had passed the first round of the selection process. Then in June of that same year she learned

Mae Carol Jemison retired from NASA after becoming the first African-American woman to travel in space and NASA's first Science Mission Specialist.

that she had been accepted into the astronaut-training program. She was only one of fifteen people chosen for the program out of the two thousand who had applied. She was also the first African-American woman ever accepted.

Jemison had to undergo an extensive twelve-month training program. She passed it and became an astronaut eligible for a space-shuttle assignment. However, it took four more years before she finally took to the air. During that time she worked for NASA and also underwent additional training.

Finally, on September 12, 1992, the space shuttle *Endeavour* took off from Florida's Kennedy Space Center. On board was a crew of seven astronauts . . . including Mae Jemison.

Mae Jemison was not only the first African-American woman to go into space, but she was also NASA's first science mission specialist.

But being first was not the reason that Jemison was so thrilled to be on *Endeavour*. As she later said, "I did always assume I would go into space, ever since I was a little girl. I was interested in going into space if a thousand people had gone before me or none had. I would still say, 'I'll go, I'll go, I'll go.'"[2]

Endeavour orbited the earth for eight days. During that time Jemison put her medical training to good use. She performed a variety of experiments in Spacelab-J, a reusable laboratory that *Endeavour* was carrying.

Some of these experiments concerned the loss of bone calcium in space, the biological effects of weightlessness, and using biofeedback, a technique used to calm oneself, as a cure for motion sickness.

Jemison also worked on a pioneering experiment that fertilized frog eggs. The experiment was conducted to see if healthy, normal frogs could grow from eggs that had been fertilized and hatched in a gravity-free environment.

During her off-duty time, Jemison enjoyed just looking out the window, seeing earth and reflecting on its beauty. She also liked listening to music, but found that weightlessness and dancing don't mix.

On September 20, 1992, *Endeavour* returned to earth. Jemison and her fellow astronauts had spent 190 hours, 30 minutes, and 23 seconds in space, while completing 127 orbits of earth.

Jemison soon found that she was just as busy on earth as she had been on the space shuttle. Her historic flight had made her a national figure. Everyone wanted to see and hear this dynamic young doctor and astronaut. Her hometown of Chicago honored her with a six-day tribute to coincide with her thirty-sixth birthday on October 17.

Once her flight was over, Jemison's name was put back into the rotation to be picked for future space missions. But in March 1993, she resigned from NASA. It was time for new challenges.

"The reason I resigned from NASA," she later said, "is I wanted to make sure that everyone was involved in where our future leads. And this technology—space exploration—is a birthright for everyone on this planet."[3]

To try and ensure that new technology does reach and benefit all the peoples of the world, Jemison formed the Jemison Group, Inc., a science and technology company based in Houston, Texas.

Some of the company's current projects are a satellite-based telecommunications system to expedite health care in West Africa, the introduction of U.S. science and literature curriculum into South Africa, and *The Earth We Share*, an international science camp.

Today, Jemison divides her time among several projects. Besides working with her company, she is a professor at Dartmouth College, New Hampshire, in the Environmental Studies Program.

In addition, Jemison is the director of the Jemison Institute for Advancing Technology in Developing Countries, which is also located at Dartmouth College. The institute's mission is to research, design, implement, and evaluate sophisticated technology to make sure that it benefits people in developing countries. In 2001, her autobiography, *Find Where the Wind Goes: Moments from My Life*, was published. She hopes her story will encourage children to follow their dreams.

No matter what she is involved in, however, Dr. Mae Jemison is still at heart the young girl who was fascinated by the wonders of science and the universe.

Jemison said, "I believe at the heart of science are the words 'I think, I wonder, and I understand'"[4] Her mission now is to make sure that humanity understands.

Chapter Notes

Chapter 1. Dorothy Lynde Dix

1. Frederick M. Herrmann, *Dorothea L. Dix and the Politics of Institutional Reform* (Trenton, N.J.: New Jersey Historical Commission, 1981), p. 7.

2. Charles Schlaifer and Lucy Freeman, *Heart's Work—Civil War Heroine & Champion of the Mentally Ill—Dorothea Lynde Dix* (New York: Paragon House, 1991), p. 29.

3. Ibid., p. 31.

4. Herrmann, p. 8.

5. Schlaifer and Freeman, p. 46.

6. Ibid., p. 42.

7. Ibid., p. 132.

8. Herrmann, p. 32.

9. Schlaifer and Freeman, p. 152.

Chapter 2. Elizabeth Blackwell

1. Hobart and William Smith Colleges, "A Persistent Rebel," *American History Illustrated,* January 1981, <http://www.hws.edu/HIS/blackwell/articles/amhistory.html> (January 21, 2002).

2. Nancy Kline, *Elizabeth Blackwell: A Doctor's Triumph* (Berkeley, Calif.: Conari Press, 1997), p. 57.

3. Ibid., p. 60.

4. Dorothy Clarke Wilson, *Lone Woman: The Story of Elizabeth Blackwell The First Woman Doctor* (Boston: Little, Brown and Company, 1970), pp. 149–150.

5. Hobart and William Smith Colleges, Margaret Munro DeLancey, "Dr. Elizabeth Blackwell's Graduation—An Eye-Witness Account" <http://www .hws.edu/his/blackwell/history/graduation.html> (January 21, 2002).

Chapter 3. Clara Barton

1. Elizabeth Brown Pryor, *Clara Barton— Professional Angel* (Philadelphia: University of Pennsylvania Press, 1987), p. 10.

2. Ibid., p. 45.

3. Stephen B. Oates, *A Woman of Valor—Clara Barton and the Civil War* (New York: The Free Press, 1994), p. 41.

4. Pryor, p. 99.

Chapter 4. Mary Edwards Walker

1. Elizabeth D. Leonard, *Yankee Women, Gender Battles in the Civil War* (New York: W. W. Norton & Company, 1994), pp. 108–109.

2. Ibid., p. 111.

3. Ibid., p. 122.

4. Ibid., p. 130.

Chapter 5. Susie King Taylor

1. Susie King Taylor, *A Black Woman's Civil War Memoirs* (New York: Markus Wiener Publishing, Inc., 1988), p. 32.

2. Ibid., pp. 40–41.

3. Ibid., p. 87.

4. Ibid., pp. 87–88.

5. Ibid., pp. 118–119.

Chapter 6. Susan LaFlesche Picotte

1. Jeri Ferris, *Native American Doctor* (Minneapolis: Carolrhoda Books, Inc., 1991), p. 39.

2. J. L. Wilkerson, A *Doctor to Her People: Dr. Susan LaFlesche Picotte* (Kansas City, Missouri: Acorn Books, 1999), p. 69.

Chapter 7. Clara Maass

1. John T. Cunningham, *Clara Maass: a Nurse, a Hospital, a Spirit* (Cedar Grove, N.J.: Rae Publishing Co. Inc., 1968), p. 41.

2. Ibid.

3. Ibid.

4. Encyclopedia Brittanica, "Women in American History," <http://women.eb.com/women/articles/Maass_Clara.html> (January 21, 2002)

5. Cunningham, p. 46.

Chapter 8. Gerty Radnitz Cori

1. Benjamin F. Shearer and Barbara S. Shearer, eds., *Notable Women in the Physical Sciences* (Westport, Conn.: Greenwood Press, 1997), p. 59.

2. Helena M. Pycior, Nancy G. Slack, and Pnina G. Abir-Am, eds., *Creative Couples in the Sciences* (New Brunswick, N.J.: Rutgers University Press, 1996), p. 75.

3. Shearer and Shearer, p. 60.

4. Pycior, et al., p. 72.

5. Ibid., p. 81.

6. Ibid., p. 83.

7. Ibid.

Chapter 9. Antonia Coello Novello

1. "Remarks at the Swearing-In Ceremony for Antonia Novello as Surgeon General," March 9, 1990, <http://bushlibrary.tamu.edu/papers/1990/90030900. html> (December 26, 2000).

2. Ibid.

3. *Dictionary of Hispanic Biography* (1996) at <http://www.galenet.com> (January 21, 2002).

4. Carol Krucoff, "Antonia Novello: A Dream Come True," *The Saturday Evening Post,* May-June 1991, p. 38.

5. "Remarks at the Swearing-In Ceremony for Antonia Novello as Surgeon General," March 9, 1990, <http://bushlibrary.tamu.edu/papers/1900/90030900.html> (January 21, 2002).

Chapter 10. Mae Carol Jemison

1. "Mae Jemison," *The Women of the Hall: National Women's Hall of Fame,* <http://www.greatwomen.org/profile.php?id=88> (June 12, 2000).

2. Michael Learmouth, "NASA as She Wants to Be," *MetroActive Features/Mae Jemison,* May 22–28, 1997, <http://www.metroactive.com/papers/metro/05.22.97/slices-9721.html> (December 11, 2000).

3. Ibid.

4. "Mae Jemison," *Apple-Applemasters,* <http://www.apple.com/applemasters/maejemison> (December 11, 2000).

Further Reading

DeAngelis, Gina. *Female Firsts in Their Fields: Science & Medicine.* Philadelphia: Chelsea House Publishers, 1999.

Fine, Edith Hope. *Barbara McClintock: Nobel Prize Geneticist.* Springfield, N.J.: Enslow Publishers, 1998.

Garza, Hedda. *Women in Medicine.* New York: Franklin Watts, 1994.

Kaye, Judith. *The Life of Florence Sabin.* New York: Twenty-First Century Books, 1993.

Kent, Jacqueline C. *Women in Medicine.* Minneapolis: Oliver Press, 1998.

Lindop, Laurie. *Scientists and Doctors.* New York: Twenty-First Century Books, 1997.

McClure, Judy. *Healers and Researchers: Physicians, Biologists, Social Scientists.* Austin, Tex.: Raintree Steck-Vaughn, 2000.

Pasternak, Ceel, and Linda Thornburg. *Cool Careers for Girls in Health.* Manassas Park, Va.: Impact Publications, 1999.

Internet Addresses

Dorothea Lynde Dix
<http://www.dhhs.state.nc.us/mhddsas/DIX/dorothea.html>

Women of the Hall: Elizabeth Blackwell
<http://www.greatwomen.org/profile.php?id=20>

Clara Barton, 1821–1912
<http://americancivilwar.com/women/cb.html>

Mary Edwards Walker: Civil War Doctor
<http://www.northnet.org/stlawrenceaauw/walker.htm>

Susie King Taylor, b. 1848
<http://docsouth.unc.edu/neh/taylorsu/menu.html>

Susan LaFlesche Picotte
<http://www.usgennet.org/usa/ne/county/thurston/susan.
   html>

Clara Maass
<http://www.stamponhistory.com/people/maass.html>

Gerty Radnitz Cori
<http://www.nobel.se/medicine/laureates/1947/cori-gt-bio.
   html>

Antonia Coello Novello
<http://www.surgeongeneral.gov/library/history/bionovello.
   htm>

Dr. Mae Carol Jemison
<http://quest.arc.nasa.gov/people/bios/women/jemison.html>

Index